Praise for *The La*

"In these pages, more than a hun ... what it is to lose someone they deeply love offer language ... meaning of this most powerful life experience. This is not a book you read once and put on a shelf. It's a precious resource to take out again and again, as life deals its inevitable blows. *The Language of Loss* looks squarely in the eye of heartbreak and offers what all of us need most: a community of voices reminding us we are not alone, and that it is possible to survive great loss and tell the story."

— **JOYCE MAYNARD**, bestselling author of
Labor Day and *The Best of Us*

"With this remarkable anthology, Barbara Abercrombie has given us solace for the soul, a companion to keep close by, for there is never a timeline for grief."

— **JACQUELINE WINSPEAR**, *New York Times* bestselling author of
the memoir *This Time Next Year We'll Be Laughing*
and the Maisie Dobbs series of historical mysteries

"A deeply moving collection of voices that intimately reveals the universal complexities of loss: how love navigates our absences, how our insurmountable grief becomes a companion, how our mourning becomes resilience."

— **RICHARD BLANCO**, 2013 presidential inaugural poet and
author of *How to Love a Country*

"We are mortal creatures who love deeply — never forget it. All great poetry is about this. And here is the anthology that proves it — simply, beautifully, tenderly, lovingly. Everyone should have at least one copy."

— **ERICA JONG**, bestselling author of *Fear of Flying*

"Here is a treasury of words for when there are no words. There is comfort here, and there are tears."

— **ABIGAIL THOMAS**, author of *A Three Dog Life*

The
Language
of Loss

Also by Barbara Abercrombie

Fiction

Good Riddance
Run for Your Life

Nonfiction

Kicking in the Wall
A Year of Writing Dangerously
Writing Out the Storm
Courage & Craft
Cherished: 21 Writers on Animals They Have Loved & Lost (editor)

Poetry

Traveling Without a Camera
(with Norma Almquist and Jeanne Nichols)

Books for Young People

The Other Side of a Poem
Amanda & Heather & Company
Cat-Man's Daughter
Michael and the Cats
Charlie Anderson
Bad Dog, Dodger!
The Show-and-Tell Lion

The Language of Loss

Poetry and Prose for Grieving
and Celebrating the Love of Your Life

Edited by

Barbara Abercrombie

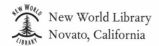 New World Library
Novato, California

New World Library
14 Pamaron Way
Novato, California 94949

Permission acknowledgements can be found beginning on page 181.

Text design by Tona Pearce Myers

Library of Congress Cataloging-in-Publication Data

Names: Abercrombie, Barbara, editor.
Title: The language of loss : poetry and prose for grieving and celebrating
    the love of your life / edited by Barbara Abercrombie.
Description: Novato, California : New World Library, 2020. | Includes
    bibliographical references and index. | Summary: "An anthology
    of noted poems and prose, both recent and classic, that deal with the
    themes of loss and grieving."-- Provided by publisher.
Identifiers: LCCN 2020030377 (print) | LCCN 2020030378 (ebook) |
    ISBN 9781608686957 (paperback) | ISBN 9781608686964 (epub)
Subjects: LCSH: Loss (Psychology)--Literary collections. | Grief--Literary
    collections.
Classification: LCC PN6071.L69 L36 2020 (print) | LCC PN6071.L69
    (ebook) | DDC 808.81/93548--dc23
LC record available at https://lccn.loc.gov/2020030377
LC ebook record available at https://lccn.loc.gov/2020030378

First printing, November 2020
ISBN 978-1-60868-695-7
Ebook ISBN 978-1-60868-696-4

Printed in the USA on 30% postconsumer-waste recycled paper

New World Library is proud to be a Gold Certified Environmentally Responsible Publisher. Publisher certification awarded by Green Press Initiative.

10   9   8   7   6   5   4   3   2   1

In memory of

Robert V. Adams, 1932–2015

When Tibor died, the world came to an end. And the world did not come to an end. That is something you learn.

—Maira Kalman

Contents

II. Going On After

III. Turning

Preface

What are the right words?

The language of condolence, no matter how well intended, irritated me. My husband had not gone to a better place as if he were off on a holiday. He had not passed like clouds overhead, nor was he my late husband as if he'd missed a train. I had not lost him as if I'd been careless, and for sure, none of it was for the best. He had died. And maybe if I heard this and said it often enough, I would finally understand that my husband had disappeared from the face of the earth and was gone forever.

I knew, of course, euphemism was offered in kindness, and I was grateful to friends for any attempt to comfort me, but what I really wanted was the language of hard truth and reality. I found myself needing to tell people over and over what had happened those final weeks. I wanted true words for his death, for what I felt. I needed to find a narrative, a story—a container for the chaos.

I told people who had not yet heard of his death that my husband had died, that my husband was dead; I was not interested in softening this news. I was learning that grief for someone you loved and shared your life with was far more complicated than I'd ever imagined it could be. I was overwhelmed not only by unspeakable sorrow and loneliness, but also with regret, guilt, confusion, and anger.

Reading always gets me through hard times, and this was the hardest of all times, but in the beginning I couldn't concentrate on prose. I needed the brevity, the cut-to-the-chase, the depth and distillation of poetry. Poems about grief in all its contradictory complications. I wanted to read poems I could relate to, poets who wrote about the death of a partner or a spouse, who could put into words my own feelings and provide "not release from grief," as Donald Hall wrote about poetry and his own grieving for his wife, "but companionship in grief."

Later, when I could concentrate again, I needed writers who turned their stories of loss and mourning into the narrative and clarity of memoir, not attempting to advise how to fix or heal grief, but telling how it felt, how they managed to get through it.

When my husband died, a recently widowed friend emailed me that if people hadn't gone through the death of a partner there was no way of explaining to them what it felt like, and if they had gone through it no explanations were necessary. A wise and dear Episcopal priest told me that I'd be crazy and fragile for a year, and then I'd still be crazy and fragile but not as much so. There are no perfect words in the face of grief, but those were the words that rang most true and guided me through the early days of being alone.

"Only grieving heals grief," wrote Anne Lamott.

Shakespeare wrote, "Give sorrow words."

After the service, after the gathering of friends, after family has flown in and then returned home, you're alone in a way you've never been before. But grief is given a short shelf life in our culture. As Madeleine L'Engle writes, "We are not good about admitting grief, we Americans. It can be embarrassing. We turn away, afraid that it might happen to us."

We the grieving are to be resilient and to pull ourselves together. We're expected to move through those stages of grief quickly, to get on with our lives and to find closure. Except there is no closure after the death of someone we love. *Closure*: a word that should only be used for roads, not hearts. You learn to live with absence. Peace and grace eventually come—but there's no closure. And our healing comes, as Jan Richardson says in her book of blessings for times of grief, "in allowing ourselves to give exquisite attention to our grief—to feel it in its terrible fullness instead of ignoring it, to let it speak instead of silencing it."

This book is about paying attention to grief, letting it speak. Language used as companionship and solace. The writers and poets in the following pages write of their loss as reality, not as euphemism, and use, as Julian Barnes writes, "the old words... death, grief, sorrow, sadness, heartbreak." Their prose and poems move from searing loss to pushing through grief with what Jane Hirshfield calls "the black clay of stubbornness going on after," and then into grace and hope, and discovering that, as Patti Smith writes, "slowly the leaves of my life turned."

As the pages and years of my own life turned, I slowly learned another language, one of gratitude. The dead do rise up and we get to keep the love we've shared with them, the story and the poetry of that love. Bashō's temple bell stops but the sound keeps going, and the world doesn't end. I learned that after grief we can find our way to rejoice in the world again, our hearts even more open than before.

PART I

Sweeping Up the Heart

The Bustle in a House

The Bustle in a House
The Morning after Death
Is solemnest of industries
Enacted opon Earth—

The Sweeping up the Heart
And putting Love away
We shall not want to use again
Until Eternity—

—EMILY DICKINSON

Even Music

Drive toward the Juan de Fuca Strait.
Listen to "Moondog Matinee."
No song ever written gets close to it:

how it feels to go on after the body
you love has been put into the ground
for eternity. Cross bridge after bridge,

through ten kinds of rain, past
abandoned fireworks booths,
their closed flaps streaked with soot.

Gash on the flank of a red barn:
Jesus Loves You. 5 $ a Fish.
He's dead. Where's your miracle?

Load a tape into the deck so a woman
can wear out a love song. Keep moving,
keep listening to the awful noise

the living make.
Even the saxophone, its blind,
unearthly moan.

—DORIANNE LAUX

FROM *Because What Else Could I Do*

I alone in a restaurant
and what is left of you at home

in a plastic box on your dresser where
you kept your socks and put your change—

and what will I do at home in my own
house, what will I do with my one

spoon and my wide bed, what
will I do without without

—MARTHA COLLINS

Funeral Blues

Stop all the clocks, cut off the telephone,
Prevent the dog from barking with the juicy bone.
Silence the pianos and with muffled drum
Bring out the coffin, let the mourners come.

Let aeroplanes circle moaning overhead
Scribbling in the sky the message He Is Dead
Put crêpe bows round the white necks of the public doves,
Let the traffic policemen wear black cotton gloves.

He was my North, my South, my East and West,
My working week and my Sunday rest,
My noon, my midnight, my talk, my song:
I thought that love would last for ever: I was wrong.

The stars are not wanted now; put out every one,
Pack up the moon and dismantle the sun,
Pour away the ocean and sweep up the wood;
For nothing now can ever come to any good.

—W. H. Auden

Time does not bring relief

Time does not bring relief; you all have lied
Who told me time would ease me of my pain!
I miss him in the weeping of the rain;
I want him at the shrinking of the tide;
The old snows melt from every mountain-side,
And last year's leaves are smoke in every lane;
But last year's bitter loving must remain
Heaped on my heart, and my old thoughts abide.
There are a hundred places where I fear
To go,—so with his memory they brim.
And entering with relief some quiet place
Where never fell his foot or shone his face
I say, "There is no memory of him here!"
And so stand stricken, so remembering him.

—EDNA ST. VINCENT MILLAY

FROM *A Grief Observed*

No one ever told me that grief felt so like fear. I am not afraid, but the sensation is like being afraid. The same fluttering in the stomach, the same restlessness, the yawning. I keep on swallowing.

At other times it feels like being mildly drunk, or concussed. There is a sort of invisible blanket between the world and me. I find it hard to take in what anyone says. Or perhaps, hard to want to take it in. It is so uninteresting. Yet I want the others to be about me. I dread the moments when the house is empty. If only they would talk to one another and not to me.

There are moments, most unexpectedly, when something inside me tries to assure me that I don't really mind so much, not so very much, after all. Love is not the whole of a man's life. I was happy before I ever met H. I've plenty of what are called "resources." People get over these things. Come, I shan't do so badly. One is ashamed to listen to this voice but it seems for a little to be making out a good case. Then comes a sudden jab of red-hot memory and all this "commonsense" vanishes like an ant in the mouth of a furnace.

On the rebound one passes into tears and pathos. Maudlin tears. I almost prefer the moments of agony. These are at least clean and honest.

—C. S. Lewis

Husband

When you left me
darkness opened
up at my feet
and I froze
just where I was,
robbed of any
destination,
lonely as the man
in a space suit,
or the deep sea diver
who must carry all his air
with him. I can't
come up too fast
or I will die of grief
blooming like a deadly gas
in my blood.
What is left here
anyway? The hills
rolled out flat
into deserts, the rivers
pulled back into the earth
leaving dry beds cracked
and crazed
like glazed china
hot from the kiln.
I will not bend.
I do not care

what rules I break.
I will stand here
and howl my loss
beneath the stony moon
until even you
will hear me.

—Mary C. McCarthy

FROM for Jane

in this room
the hours of love
still make shadows.

when you left
you took almost
everything.

I kneel in the nights
before tigers
that will not let me be.

what you were
will not happen again.

the tigers have found me
and I do not care.

—CHARLES BUKOWSKI

from Death Poem

I can close my eyes and sit back if I want to,
I can lean against my friends' shoulders
and eat as they're eating, and drink from the bottle
being passed back and forth; I can lighten up, can't I,
Christ, can't I? There is another subject, in a minute
I'll think of it. I will. And if you know it, help me.
Help me. Remind me why I'm here.

—KIM ADDONIZIO

Lemon and cedar

What is so pure as grief? A wreck
set sail just to be wrecked again.
To lose what's lost—it's all born lost
and we just fetch it for a little while,
a dandelion span, a quarter-note.
Each day an envelope gummed shut
with honey and mud. Foolish
to think you can build a house
from suffering. Even the hinges will be
bitter. There will be no books
in that house, only transfusions.
And all the lemon and cedar
in the world won't rid the walls
of that hospital smell.

—MELISSA STEIN

The Role of Elegy

The role of elegy is
To put a mask on tragedy,
A drape on the mirror.
To bow to the cultural

Debate over the anesthetization of sorrow,
Of loss, of the unbearable
Afterimage of the once material.
To look for an imagined

Consolation of grief
So we can all be finished
Once and for all and genuinely shut up
The cabinet of genuine particulars.

Instead there's the endless refrain
One hears replayed repeatedly
Through the just ajar door:
Some terrible mistake has been made.

What is elegy but the attempt
To rebreathe life
Into what the gone one once was
Before he grew to enormity.

Come on stage and be yourself,
The elegist says to the dead. Show them

Now—after the fact—
What you were meant to be:

The performer of a live song.
A shoe. Now bow.
What is left is this:
The compulsion to tell.

The transient distraction of ink on cloth
One scrubbed and scrubbed
But couldn't make less
Not then, not soon.

Each day, a new caption on the cartoon
Ending that simply cannot be.
One hears repeatedly, the role of elegy is.

—MARY JO BANG

Spell to Bring a Dead Husband Back

Come back to me and fetch your busted heart.

Come back to me and take the medications
       the doctors said would make you well

Come back to me and save me from
       this guilt over not saving you

Come back to me and call your mother—
       she's lonely for the sound
       of your voice

Come back to me and read me your
       poems—I can read them
       but it's better if you read them
       because you wrote them
       and I'm only a spectator

Come back to me and take your place
       in this bed that I've filled
       with books and clothes and
       condolence cards, as if
       their weight could replicate yours
       their heft not resembling
       the bones and body I slept beside

Come back to me and fight me
        for the remote

Come back—let me feed you
Come back—let me rub your sore
        shoulder with CBD
        in the hope it would loosen
        and you could start another day
        put on another blue shirt
        from your closet of blue shirts

Come back, come back, come back
        with your glasses precariously
        on your nose; you'd push them
        back with fingers you called
        stubby

Come back and find your wedding ring
        your pocket change
        your heavy fist of office keys
        your money under the welcome mat
        your pens in a secret drawer

Come back, come back, come back,
        I say, as I rock my body
        into that cursed sleep

Come back through the flames and the urns
the platitudes and the eulogies

Come back and we will all
      the pleasures prove,
      stopping the clocks and
        the calendars

Come back, come back, come back—damn it—come back.

—ALLISON JOSEPH

FROM *Levels of Life*

I did already know that only the old words would do: death, grief, sorrow, sadness, heartbreak. Nothing modernly evasive or medicalising. Grief is a human, not a medical, condition, and while there are pills to help us forget it—and everything else—there are no pills to cure it. The griefstruck are not depressed, just properly, appropriately, mathematically ("it hurts exactly as much as it is worth") sad. One euphemistic verb I especially loathed was "pass." "I'm sorry to hear your wife has passed" (as in "passed water"? "passed blood"?). You do not have to force the word "die" on others, even if you always use it yourself. There is a midpoint. At a social event she and I would normally have attended together, an acquaintance came up and said to me, simply, "There's someone missing." That felt correct, in both senses.

—JULIAN BARNES

Rising

I swear I saw you leave—
bereft of words, feet dangling

above ground as though
deprived of bone and sinew,

light shining through
your worn garments.

Never again can I angle
against you, reattach

a button to your jacket.
You are gathered elsewhere,

alone and emptied. I see that,
the way, sometimes, one can

hear the end of a word before
its completion.

—JACQUELINE DERNER TCHAKALIAN

FROM *Mother Daughter Me*

The autopsy showed a near-total occlusion in the left anterior descending artery, a major supplier of blood to the heart and a conduit so vital that physicians often refer to such a blockage as "the widow-maker." It was unclear how long his heart had been diseased, but I blamed myself. I blamed myself for causing him stress during our bad patch. I blamed myself for not picking up on his fatigue or any other small symptoms he might have shown. I blamed myself for not probing a little more on the day before he died, when he called and sounded agitated. I would blame myself for years to come.

—KATIE HAFNER

FROM *Grieving: A Love Story*

I am distracted, disoriented, disconnected, pacing the house in circles, mindlessly retracing my steps over and over again.... One afternoon I finally force myself to go looking for a new bed; it is my first and only outing toward that end, and it is an unmitigated disaster. I cannot believe I am doing this. I cannot believe I am talking to an overzealous salesman about buying a king-sized bed, which in itself sounds to me like a berserk act....

It is apparent that I cannot seriously think about buying a new bed. I cannot think about anything except the irrefutable fact that Bill is dead. The realization, which has been strangely slow in coming to me, death certificate and all—that I will never see him again, that I will never hear his voice again, that he is extinct—hits me like a roundhouse punch. I am on the ropes and there is no one here to get me back on my feet.

—RUTH COUGHLIN

Refractory

The Stages of Grief:

> Denial
>
> Anger
>
> Bargaining
>
> Depression
>
> Acceptance

I cannot let go, cannot
follow the protocol, refuse
closure, refuse to doubt you
are about to slip back through
a loophole, undo the tricked-out
trickery of the spring your heart shut
down in the willful green of the thick
coming grass. I rage at you now as I did
not rage then. How could you
have left me to the futile pink
of the Red Bud preening
like a buffoon through the glass
of our bedroom window? Look:
I stand ready to make a deal.
Take what you need, then call it quits
with eternity. I know you grieve, too.
I will never ask another indulgence
from whatever it is we end by
calling upon *in extremis*. But you do
not, will not, did not, come back

for all this time I pass confounding
assumptions, eluding the rules
for healthy adjustment and getting on
with the rest of it I still cannot accept.

—CAROL TUFTS

What It's Like

imagine the earthquake—

it's possible,
eventually
the big one
we all know
is coming to California
we should get ready
be prepared
the water, the food
flashlights and batteries

and some of us do that
make our little plans
to be brave and resourceful
to survive
the foundation cracking
the walls crumbling
the windows shattering

you think you know what it will be like
but you have no idea

when the walls begin to wail

and peel away from the house

when you can't find your shoes or the dog

when shattered glass shreds your feet

when the air turns red

with sirens

when your world

dims black into loss

the foundation not cracked

but buried—

unimaginable

but possible

and it will be like nothing you've ever known

it will be like grief

—Barbara Abercrombie

Sonnet 23

Methought I saw my late espoused saint
    Brought to me like Alcestis from the grave,
    Whom Jove's great son to her glad husband gave,
    Rescued from Death by force, though pale and faint.
Mine, as whom washed from spot of child-bed taint
    Purification in the old Law did save,
    And such as yet once more I trust to have
    Full sight of her in heaven without restraint,
Came vested all in white, pure as her mind.
    Her face was veiled; yet to my fancied sight
    Love, sweetness, goodness, in her person shined
So clear as in no face with more delight.
    But O as to embrace me she inclined,
    I waked, she fled, and day brought back my night.

—JOHN MILTON

After Her Death

I am trying to find the lesson
for tomorrow. Matthew something.
Which lectionary? I have not
forgotten the Way, but, a little,
the way to the Way. The trees keep whispering
peace, peace, and the birds
in the shallows are full of the
bodies of small fish and are
content. They open their wings
so easily, and fly. So. It is still
possible.

       I open the book
which the strange, difficult, beautiful church
has given me. To Matthew. Anywhere.

—MARY OLIVER

The Sadness of Clothes

When someone dies, the clothes are so sad. They have outlived
their usefulness and cannot get warm and full.
You talk to the clothes and explain that he is not coming back

as when he showed up immaculately dressed in slacks and plaid
     jacket
and had that beautiful smile on and you'd talk.
You'd go to get something and come back and he'd be gone.

You explain death to the clothes like that dream.
You tell them how much you miss the spouse
and how much you miss the pet with its little winter sweater.

You tell the worn raincoat that if you talk about it,
you will finally let grief out. The ancients etched the words
for battle and victory onto their shields and then they went out

and fought to the last breath. Words have that kind of power
you remind the clothes that remain in the drawer, arms
     stubbornly
folded across the chest, or slung across the backs of chairs,

or hanging inside the dark closet. Do with us what you will,
they faintly sigh, as you close the door on them.
He is gone and no one can tell us where.

—EMILY FRAGOS

FROM *Insomniac City*

In those early days of grief, short on sleep, forgetting to eat, I felt as though I were in a liminal state, not quite alive myself, which made me feel remarkably close to Steve. During that same period, I was continually having amazing encounters with strangers—people who would pop up and offer help, whether at the post office or grocery store, or just say something kind. At the time, I never doubted that they were embodiments of him.

One day I met a man with the name of an angel. He was French. His accent was so thick it sounded fake. We got to talking and I told him what had happened. "You're going to be fine," Emmanuel said right away. "Something bad always leads to something good." He spoke from personal experience. His partner had died six years earlier. But he did not use that word, *died*, as he told me his story. Nor did he say *passed away*, a euphemism I had come to hate. Instead, Emmanuel said, "When my partner disappeared…"

I knew this was not a case of poor English, a bungled translation. Still, I had to say something. "You said 'disappeared'—"

He nodded.

"That's exactly how it feels for me, too."

—BILL HAYES

Ovation

I try to make myself afraid,
the way you must have been afraid,
stepping out onto this stage—
but with a fear so pure, so

perfectly informed that you strode
out shouting. Here, where
the neon yellow arrows painted
on the floor shoot forward underfoot

in blackness—beneath the hanging
sequence of tinted skies—out toward
that mindless immortalizing light, now
dark. Now I think I feel the heat you

must have felt rising from the front rows.
A gaping fire door, a furnace:
your single body standing here
with no shadow, swinging on itself.

Had you been a fool, you might have thought
that they loved you. They never love you,
you said. They are hungry for the god
in his gold eclipse, the pure you on fire.

John and I move quickly, each with a handful
of ash, scattering. The sound of no sound falling

into the cracks in the boards, the footlights,
the first row. A small personal snow: a prince

of dust, a villain of dust. Each part you played
drifting up again, recomposing. I open my hand,
I let you go—back into the lines you learned,
back into the body and the body's beauty—

back into the standing ovation: bow after bow after bow.

—CAROL MUSKE-DUKES

FROM *The Best Day the Worst Day*

Everything I did, those first weeks and months, I did deliberately, with lunatic clarity and without judgment. Before driving home that day, for no reason, I visited the new Concord Wal-Mart. I pushed a cart around and bought nothing. *Who am I and what am I doing here?* When I turned the cart into one aisle I suddenly wept. It was office supplies—pads and pens, Post-its, clasped envelopes—writerly objects that Jane and I had given each other as tokens of affection. When I returned from a trip, I might bring Jane a package of fancy striped paper clips; when Jane came back from a poetry reading, she might hand me a lined pad with Elvis on the cover. Driving home from Wal-Mart, I suffered the onslaught of a new emotion; I felt intense, overwhelming, permeating shame. I remember it still, the way one remembers certain nightmares. I drowned under shame's ocean, crying and heartsick as I drove up I-93. No thought or recollection set me off. What did I feel shame for? For letting her die? It reminded me of one thing only: waking in the morning, twenty-five years earlier in Michigan, desolate between marriages; I had been drunk the night before, and knew I had done something unspeakable but had no notion of what I had done.

—Donald Hall

33

To Ashes

A tisket a tasket
they've put him in a casket
to ship him off our island
to burn his spirit free.

Standing in the deep sand
(quicksand) near the ferry
I'm distracted for the hour
by such absurdity.

Autumn summons winter.
There is no way back.
The trees will bare at sunrise,
the birds all black.

—Rose Styron

FROM *A Severe Mercy*

The grim and almost fierce will to do all and be all for Davy that I had held before me like a sword for half a year became now, upon her death, tired though I was, a no less resolute will to face the whole meaning of loss, to drink the cup of grief to the lees. I came, thereby, to see something of the nature of loss and grief.

First there were the immediate duties...the sowing of the ashes. And I would face the grief alone; I would not show it before others....

The next day I taught my classes. By then I had written some sixty letters, each one ending: "And in Davy's words: 'All shall be most well.'" I caused it to be known that I did not want condolence calls, and I believe some people thought me callous....I went through her things like a storm—a sorrowing storm....

I could smile, too. And I was conscious of a sort of amazement that the sky was still blue and a steak still tasted good. How could things go *on* when the world had come to an end? How could things—how could *I*—go on in this void? How could one person, not very big, leave an emptiness that was galaxy-wide?

—SHELDON VANAUKEN

God putting on a show of tenderness, nothing like thoughts
that rise and drift in my mind, like flakes shaken
in a snow globe, and my brain laboring in its own night,
never feeling the punky starlight of dark thirty, the time
a friend said for us to meet and had to explain it was half an hour
after the first dark, when daylilies fold up and headlights
lead the way home, but maybe too early
to find the moon turning half its body away,
holding it hidden like the black side of a mirror, unseen
until it breaks, unexpectedly, the way grief
breaks over you when you've already given all you've got
and hands you tools you don't know how to use.

—BARBARA RAS

FROM *The Widower's Notebook*

I could not locate nor separate my feelings of grief from guilt, nor guilt from loss, nor sadness from depression—all of those feelings roiling around, though guilt often managed to find its way to the surface and ride the waves.

The flip side of guilt is self-pity.

It's the danger inherent in all grieving, feeling sorry for yourself. On occasion, I can separate my sorrow from self-pity, but the two play a good game of catch and at worst go hand in hand. It's hard, once you've allowed yourself to go down the self-pity road, to do an about-face because wallowing in self-pity is such sweet agony. And yet, the idea of anyone feeling sorry for me is truly abhorrent. Remember, I am, and was, very busy keeping up all appearances of manly reserve.

Guilt was hard to avoid and get over, and it still, on occasion, crawls inside my head and whispers all sorts of bad stuff. The only thing I can do is not listen.

And yet, one needs to listen, to pay attention, because there are important things to be heard, and to be done. However painful, it's better to be at least partially conscious, to feel the pain rather than pretend it's not happening. Better to have painful memories than to have no memories at all.

—JONATHAN SANTLOFER

Precision

The day you flew in perfect arc
from your motorcycle was the same day
I broke the perfect formation of your women
at the railing, leaving behind
your grandmother and mother, to run
and jump the fence. The stop watch hanging
from my neck, suspended between gravity
and momentum, swung its flawless pendulum.

All our motion was brought to conclusion
by your broken body at rest
on the ground. Your breath never rose
to the oxygen placed on your face
and your heart never rallied
to the arms pressing your chest.
You wore the perfect clothes:
the ashy grey of death.

At the hospital they said your failure to survive
was complete. Though I never saw
the neck you perfectly broke or your body
cleanly draped by a sheet, I did see
your dead face bruising up at me
and for lack of something moving to touch,
I clutched the stop watch
which had not died.

Had any nurse or doctor asked,
I could have told, exactly,
to the hundredths of seconds, how long
it had been since I'd seen you alive.

—Laurie Duesing

FROM Poof!

Death, as Julian Barnes put it, is "just the universe doing its stuff," and it did its stuff to Leon at 4:58 on Sunday morning, 25 August 2013.

He was here. Now he's not.

He was somewhere. Now he's nowhere.

He was alive. Now he's dead.

He loved me. Now he doesn't.

We shared a personal language, a dictionary of intimacy. That language is now obsolete.

I know his face better than my own because I looked at it every single day for the thirty-seven years we were together. I'll never see that face again.

I'll never touch or kiss or feel his body.

He hasn't passed away, because that presupposes he's passed away to some other place.

Nor...did I lose him—that presupposes there's a chance, however slim, of my being able to find him.

He just died.

Ceased to exist.

Disappeared.

—AVIVA LAYTON

FROM And Thou Art Dead, as Young and Fair

Yet did I love thee to the last
    As fervently as thou,
Who didst not change through all the past,
    And canst not alter now.
The love where Death has set his seal,
Nor age can chill, nor rival steal,
    Nor falsehood disavow :
And, what were worse, thou canst not see
Or wrong, or change, or fault in me.

The better days of life were ours ;
    The worst can be but mine :
The sun that cheers, the storm that lowers,
    Shall never more be thine.
The silence of that dreamless sleep
I envy now too much to weep ;
    Nor need I to repine
That all those charms have pass'd away,
I might have watch'd through long decay.

The flower in ripen'd bloom unmatch'd
    Must fall the earliest prey ;
. . . .
As once I wept, if I could weep,
    My tears might well be shed,
To think I was not near to keep
    One vigil o'er thy bed ;

To gaze, how fondly ! on thy face,
To fold thee in a faint embrace,
    Uphold thy drooping head ;
And show that love, however vain,
Nor thou nor I can feel again.

Yet how much less it were to gain,
    Though thou hast left me free,
The loveliest things that still remain,
    Than thus remember thee !
The all of thine that cannot die
Through dread and dark Eternity
    Returns again to me,
And more thy buried love endears
Than aught, except its living years.

—LORD BYRON

FROM Against the Current

I think of calling

Your office number

Just to see

If your voice

Is still there

On the voicemail

A disembodied voice

But I can't

And when I try

A week later

It's gone

—MATT BIALER

The Year After

In the year after our life ended,
When you put a gun to your head,
In the year that my eyes turned to glass,
That my heart turned to iron,
Only my hands remained human.

They seized the axe for firewood,
The hoe to loosen hard soil,
The knife to prepare the evening meal,
The shears to cut flowers, beauty
Indifferent to its own decay.

Only my hands continued human,
Writing red on student themes,
Writing black on the white pages
Of emptiness. The only tears were black,
The cries were only lines joined to lines.

My shaping hands held up this semblance
Of structure, pulse, and picture
To my eyes of glass, my iron heart.
Dazed Galatea of my own poems
I stepped down from death.

—Virginia Hamilton Adair

He Is Trying to Get Home
from the Store,

but lake winds pick him up
& blow him into the clouds. I
married a dreamer. I wait. He
stops to listen to the early
lilac orchestra. He starts to
change into blowy horizontal lake
rain, then migrating red admirals.

I thinksay remember. I remember us.
We chose the imaginal
north/south somewhere
between Bartlett Avenue and Jupiter,
between Lake Michigan and
the Aegean. Remember we drink
Serbian Cosmos together, we eat
squash blossoms and red snapper soup.
We visit the Calatrava before bed. We
nurture a magnetic field of words. I am

remembering you back. Remembering
plays time. Thinking is all remembering.
I remember our young
bodies. I'm not finished
with us. Remember that.
If someone asks, "why is that lady
out walking in that lake storm?" Tell them

"months ago her husband went to the
store in a blizzard & never came back."
Tell them: "She can't stop looking for him."

—SUSAN FIRER

FROM consummation of grief

I even hear the mountains
the way they laugh
up and down their blue sides
and down in the water
the fish cry
and all the water
is their tears.
I listen to the water
on nights I drink away
and the sadness becomes so great
I hear it in my clock
it becomes knobs upon my dresser
it becomes paper on the floor
it becomes a shoehorn
a laundry ticket
it becomes
cigarette smoke
climbing a chapel of dark vines...

—CHARLES BUKOWSKI

FROM A Widow's First Five Years

And then came the silence in the wake of his death.

The silence of grief is not silent. The silence of grief is the absence of the beloved's presence. And into that silence comes the keening.

After a month I went to speak to a woman I could trust to tell me the truth. How long would I feel like this? I wanted to know. I wanted a straight answer, not one given to make me feel better. . . . "How long will it hurt this much?" I asked. I described a feeling of being without skin, a body of raw nerve endings. And inside those nerve endings was a wind tunnel. The wind howled day and night. Grief is as dramatically physical as it is emotional. I felt, I explained, as though I were walking naked in a cold, gray, empty world with nothing but fear as a companion.

"Expect five bad years," she said.

I was shocked. How could I survive five years?

And then, in the fashion of a child stamping her feet, I protested, "I haven't got five years to put into this." I was a relatively young widow. It seemed wrong not to get on with my life. Soon.

Patience, I was to learn, is the first requirement for safe travel out of grief's domain.

—Barbara Lazear Ascher

FROM Grief

Trying to remember you
is like carrying water
in my hands a long distance
across sand. Somewhere
people are waiting.
They have drunk nothing for days.

Your name was the food I lived on;
now my mouth is full of dirt and ash.
To say your name was to be surrounded
by feathers and silk; now, reaching out,
I touch glass and barbed wire.
Your name was the thread connecting my life;
now I am fragments on a tailor's floor.

—STEPHEN DOBYNS

Elegy for a Man and a House

Everything in my voice: antique.
It cracks like the static of your sleep
the last time you rolled over,
away, curls into something older
than wood, frame, this empty square:
roof, door, a wall to measure
how and why we grow, windows
slit like an eye on the side of the moon
that caught us young, let go
before your breath dipped, stopped.
Oh, Giacomo, though it's winter
and this rough floor cold,
I walk with my shoes off
to catch your splinters.

—Marjorie Maddox

Coats

I saw him leaving the hospital
with a woman's coat over his arm.
Clearly she would not need it.
The sunglasses he wore could not
Conceal his wet face, his bafflement.

As if in mockery the day was fair,
and the air mild for December. All the same
he had zipped his own coat and tied
the hood under his chin, preparing
for irremediable cold.

—JANE KENYON

Grief Without Fantasy

What I lost
was not going to happen.

I had
what happened.

There was no more.

—RONNA BLOOM

One Way or Another

She is gone, where did she go?
He can't imagine how the house will feel
when he enters it, moving room to room.
Now that the wait is over, a larger pause
will blanket the roof, softness settling
slowly down. By which window or door
may future days enter? And what about minor
questions called out, to which there was always
that lilting reply?

—NAOMI SHIHAB NYE

FROM Writing the Impossible Grief of Young Widowhood

I was resolutely alone: I didn't want to be comforted, but to be smart enough to make sense of what was happening to me, and to have the grit to confront it. I sensed, too, that just as I had no model for this experience, neither did the people around me. Bryan's death disrupted the order of things, gestured at a lawless void. Some friends sent apologies but didn't come to the funeral. Others slipped away without excuse. I unnerved people. They didn't know what to make of me.

In books and film, a dead partner in the approach to middle age lends itself to the poignancy of sad children drawing pictures and saying things about heaven, of wedding photos on mantels. Older, it's the territory of cancer and heart attacks, the invariably failing body. In your twenties, though, the loss of a partner can only have happened by the most unnatural of causes. Young grief is rare and obscene.

A friend from college sent a Facebook message asking if there was anything she and her husband could do for me. After the offer, she added, *You're living my worst nightmare.* I suppose the situation called for me to comfort her—*oh don't worry,* I could've said, *you'll never be so unlucky*—but I didn't respond. A few weeks later, I noticed she'd unfriended me. My notifications pinged with another message from a high school classmate. *I knew what happened, but I didn't know what to say to you. I felt sorry for you, though,* she said.

These messages were sent by people who liked me and who were doing what was polite, I think. I was meant to feel seen.

Instead they reflected my image back to me through a funhouse mirror: distorted, a ghoulish spectacle. *I don't want to be rude*, these messages said. *But you terrify me.*

—KELSEY RONAN

A Wife's Grief Because of Her Husband's Absence

The falcon swiftly seeks the north,
And forest gloom that sent it forth.
Since I no more my husband see,
My heart from grief is never free.
O how is it, I long to know,
That he, my lord, forgets me so?

Bushy oaks on the mountain grow,
And six elms where the ground is low.
But I, my husband seen no more,
My sad and joyless fate deplore.
O how is it, I long to know,
That he, my lord, forgets me so?

The hills the bushy wild plums show,
And pear-trees grace the ground below.
But, with my husband from me gone,
As drunk with grief, I dwell alone.
O how is it, I long to know,
That he, my lord, forgets me so?

—CONFUCIUS

FROM *Standby*

I remember the word now they used for dying. It was *pass*.

Such presumption on their part. Passing on to what, where? My husband's dying was no slight shift of place. It was a shock, a tragedy, a fracturing of so many of our dreams, our assumptions, our future. The fact of my husband's death, anyone's death, calls for the chords of a grand Bach cantata, the stomp and blare of a New Orleans jazz funeral, not the silent, stealth-like, smooth-seamed sound of a word like *pass*. Please pass the butter. The offertory plate gets passed in church. These are horizontal actions. A football pass has an arc, but the ball lands again. Death is not horizontal. There is no arc that returns to earth. The fact of death the moment you learn, know that someone you love has died, if one was to choose a word implying movement, it might be that death is a shattering, or explosion, annihilation. The anima of the physical body is gone, never to return. Gone. The flesh is still. Blood no longer flows. There is a rip, a tear, a break so sudden and large and final that you lose your breath, your reality, your feelings.

—Sandy Broyard

FROM *I Dreamed of Africa*

I will not forget the smell of gardenia, and the feel of the fleshy petals on my clutching fingers, the day we flew Paolo's body back home to bury him....

The night he died, I wrote to him until morning. I chose to say now the simplest words. I did not have much voice....

Your eyes were the colour of water:
Yes, you are water.

They had the transparencies of air:
Yes, you are this sky now.

Your skin was baked by the sun
like Kenya's earth:
yes, you are this red dry dust.

Forever, forever, forever, Paolo,
you have become everything.

These were my words of requiem, and I crumpled the sheet of paper and threw it in the open grave, together with what was left of that gardenia. It fell gently and noiselessly, like a feather.

—KUKI GALLMANN

Passing Is Temporary

Yes, I know he's dead—
but I'm going to say *passed*
right now because I need
to say that softer word—
not because I don't know
my husband is dead.
I saw his body before his body
became ash; I saw his hands
settled on his chest, weighty,
weightless. I saw his bruised
and silent face, blood stilled
beneath skin dotted and spotted,
familiar constellations now cold.
To say *passed* to ease my way
down this pathway of grief,
this haze of sleeplessness
and thwarted tears—sorry
not sorry if euphemism
makes you uncomfortable—
go roll your eyes at my
clichés away from me.
My love is passed,
gone, deceased, but not
ceased from my febrile
imagination, all the fever

dreams that I crave eluding
me, the hiss of silence and self-
talk my newest reality.

—ALLISON JOSEPH

FROM Sixteenth Anniversary

You died early and in summer.

Before heading to the cemetery
I made them leave the lid up
while I ran out to the garden
and picked one more bouquet
of sweet peas to fan onto your
chest, remembering how you
beamed when I placed them
on your writing desk in
the mornings. You'd draw
the scent in deeply,
then I'd kiss you on the brow,
go out, and quietly close
the door.

We survive on ritual, on
sweet peas in August, letting
the scent carry us, so at last the door
swings open and we're both
on the same side of it
for a while.

—TESS GALLAGHER

FROM *The Iceberg*

It was snowing on the day we buried you: small flakes, wide-spaced, tugged hard by the wind. Unplanned, we formed a circle around your grave and stood as the words went up. Your child and his friends were everywhere present in our procession, threading lightly through the lines of mourners. I scatter earth over you and so does he, fingers splayed back, palm flat. You have moved through us and now you are gone, leaving us standing. And so are the living comforted.

—MARION COUTTS

FROM *The Pure Lover*

All feeling and all thought, all, are absent in your absence, so why, why is such total absence of thought and feeling so potent a presence—yours?

The closer I get to the final feeling, the final thought about you dead, the very feeling, the very thought, turns itself as not the final feeling, not the final thought.

Let loose, I tell myself, let loose all that I feel, let loose all that I feel into grief, and, oh, let that grief expand and expand and expand, so beyond me that grief ceases to be mine.

—DAVID PLANTE

PART II

Going On After

from Rebus

You work with what you are given,
the red clay of grief,
the black clay of stubbornness going on after.

—Jane Hirshfield

How It Will Happen, When

There you are, exhausted from another night of crying,
curled up on the couch, the floor, at the foot of the bed,

anywhere you fall you fall down crying, half amazed
at what the body is capable of, not believing you can cry

anymore. And there they are: his socks, his shirt, your
underwear, and your winter gloves, all in a loose pile

next to the bathroom door, and you fall down again.
Someday, years from now, things will be different:

the house clean for once, everything in its place, windows
shining, sun coming in easily now, skimming across

the thin glaze of wax on the wood floor. You'll be peeling
an orange or watching a bird leap from the edge of the rooftop

next door, noticing how, for an instant, her body is trapped
in the air, only a moment before gathering the will to fly

into the ruff at her wings, and then doing it: flying.
You'll be reading, and for a moment you'll see a word

you don't recognize, a simple word like cup or gate or wisp
and you'll ponder it like a child discovering language.

Cup, you'll say it over and over until it begins to make sense,
and that's when you'll say it, for the first time, out loud: He's
  dead.

He's not coming back, and it will be the first time you believe it.

—DORIANNE LAUX

Wait

Wait, for now.
Distrust everything if you have to.
But trust the hours. Haven't they
carried you everywhere, up to now?
Personal events will become interesting again.
Hair will become interesting.
Pain will become interesting.
Buds that open out of season will become interesting.
Second-hand gloves will become lovely again;
their memories are what give them
the need for other hands. And the desolation
of lovers is the same: that enormous emptiness
carved out of such tiny beings as we are
asks to be filled; the need
for the new love is faithfulness to the old.

Wait.
Don't go too early.
You're tired. But everyone's tired.
But no one is tired enough.
Only wait a little and listen:
music of hair,
music of pain,
music of looms weaving all our loves again.
Be there to hear it, it will be the only time,
most of all to hear
the flute of your whole existence,
rehearsed by the sorrows, play itself into total exhaustion.

—GALWAY KINNELL

Dos Gardenias

I need to tell you how days drag now
that you're gone; no phone calls or Skype.

The light is never bright or warm. No one
wants to dance. Today I emptied an old bottle

of your pills, packed it with Hindu Kush,
drove to the beach. Lit up.

It's legal now in California.

I play your favorite music: Buena Vista
Social Club, Ibrahim Ferrer.

Remember that yellow bikini you used to wear?
It made you look invincible, like a star.

I'd wear the Che Guevara cap you brought
from Cuba when we danced, girl on girl
to *Dos Gardenias*. Our song.

Your breasts crushing mine.
Those signature gardenias pinned in your hair.

Now I dance alone, my screen dark.
I will not weep. You'd hate it.

Since you died, I play *Dos Gardenias*
every day, and the way the palm trees sway
breaks my heart.

You're out there, dancing,
aren't you?

Your yellow bikini a beacon, if only I could find it
in the star-crossed night.

—ALEXIS RHONE FANCHER

One Art

The art of losing isn't hard to master;
so many things seem filled with the intent
to be lost that their loss is no disaster.

Lose something every day. Accept the fluster
of lost door keys, the hour badly spent.
The art of losing isn't hard to master.

Then practice losing farther, losing faster:
places, and names, and where it was you meant
to travel. None of these will bring disaster.

I lost my mother's watch. And look! my last, or
next-to-last, of three loved houses went.
The art of losing isn't hard to master.

I lost two cities, lovely ones. And, vaster,
some realms I owned, two rivers, a continent.
I miss them, but it wasn't a disaster.

—Even losing you (the joking voice, a gesture
I love) I shan't have lied. It's evident
the art of losing's not too hard to master
though it may look like (*Write* it!) like disaster.

—ELIZABETH BISHOP

FROM Pushing Through

It's possible I am pushing through solid rock
in flintlike layers, as the ore lies, alone;
I am such a long way in I see no way through,
and no space: everything is close to my face,
and everything close to my face is stone.
I don't have much knowledge yet in grief
so this massive darkness makes me small.

—RAINER MARIA RILKE
Translated from the German by Robert Bly

FROM The River

Dan not only sent messages after he died, he visited me in dreams. He has assured me that he's doing fine and that there are parties and music in this place beyond the living. In our dream world he's traded his jeans and Costco tee-shirts for boleros, designer sunglasses, and stylish leather jackets; and we've traveled more—a camping trip in a spectacular canyon, a visit to a magnificent library, and a festival where the sky was full of men fashioned from balloons. In one dream we laid out a plan for how to make contact when he returns in another body. "Bruges will be my new name," he said. A friend told me that *bruge* means bridge, but I don't know what to make of any of this, except that sometimes the new name slips from my mind, and my heart pounds until I remember it....

...When I last dreamed of Dan we were at a party. He pulled up a chair across from me, our knees nearly touching. "You're back," I said, setting down my drink. I took his face in my hands and our eyes locked.

"You know I can't stay," he said.

—DENISE EMANUEL CLEMEN

Blessing for the Brokenhearted

There is no remedy for love but to love more.
    —HENRY DAVID THOREAU

Let us agree
for now
that we will not say
the breaking
makes us stronger
or that it is better
to have this pain
than to have done
without this love.

Let us promise
we will not
tell ourselves
time will heal
the wound,
when every day
our waking
opens it anew.

Perhaps for now
it can be enough
to simply marvel
at the mystery
of how a heart

so broken
can go on beating,
as if it were made
for precisely this—

as if it knows
the only cure for love
is more of it,

as if it sees
the heart's sole remedy
for breaking
is to love still,

as if it trusts
that its own
persistent pulse
is the rhythm
of a blessing
we cannot
begin to fathom
but will save us
nonetheless.

—JAN RICHARDSON

Companion

When Grief came to visit,
she hung her skirts and jackets in my closet.
She claimed the one bath.

When I protested,
she assured me it would be
only for a little while.

Then she fell in love with the house,
re-papered the rooms,
laid green carpet in the den.

She's a good listener
and a fiend at double solitaire.
But it's been seven years.

Once I ordered her outright to leave.
Days later
she came back, weeping.

I'd enjoyed my mornings,
coffee for one,
my Tolstoy and Molière.

I asked her in.

—Jo McDougall

FROM *Standby*

Eight months and four days. I am alone and empty in a way that I wasn't before. It's as if I'm beginning to wake up to the reality of my new life and it frightens me. Having the new puppy is a distraction, but it also reminds me that the fullness of our family will never again be the way it was. There is a thinness now. I don't have it in me to provide the food, the order, the cleanliness, the assurance that home is a stable place where you come and get refueled. I am tottering on the edge of my own existence and toying with all sorts of catastrophes.

I cry every day now. It's not that I mind all the crying. The wetness and feelings will pass. What troubles me is the brooding sadness. It feels like a dampness creeping into my life, accompanied by mold. I fear that the edges of the shapes that are familiar to me will turn limp and musty green. The house looks as if it has gotten beyond the point of sorting and arranging. Comments about the Collyer brothers are no longer funny. The upheaval is too real. Am I a collaborator? Do I languish in this state of grief, of mess, of being lost? The ongoing grief, is it a way of being loyal to Anatole, staying close to him by sinking into this mire?

—SANDY BROYARD

Waking Instructions

Crawl ashore
to the damp beginning of day.

Forget before and after.

Allow yourself
to be spelled differently.

It will feel like falling.

It has waiting attached.

—EMMA MELLON

FROM *AfterImage*

I am reading a book, but what I am really doing is grieving. I am talking to a friend over lunch, but what I am really doing is grieving. I am watching a movie, but what I am really doing is grieving. I look like I'm in motion—I *am* in motion—but what I really am, deep at my core, is still. Frozen. *Kine*—for motion. *Stasis*—for still.

—CARLA MALDEN

The Five Stages of Grief

The night I lost you
someone pointed me towards
The Five Stages of Grief.
Go that way, they said,
it's easy, like learning to climb
stairs after the amputation.
And so I climbed.
Denial was first.
I sat down at breakfast
carefully setting the table
for two. I passed you the toast—
you sat there. I passed
you the paper—you hid
behind it.
Anger seemed more familiar.
I burned the toast, snatched
the paper and read the headlines myself.
But they mentioned your departure,
and so I moved on to
Bargaining. What could I exchange
for you? The silence
after storms? My typing fingers?
Before I could decide, *Depression*
came puffing up, a poor relation
its suitcase tied together
with string. In the suitcase
were bandages for the eyes

and bottles of sleep. I slid
all the way down the stairs
feeling nothing.
And all the time Hope
flashed on and off
in defective neon.
Hope was a signpost pointing
straight in the air.
Hope was my uncle's middle name,
he died of it.
After a year I am still climbing,
though my feet slip
on your stone face.
The treeline
has long since disappeared;
green is a color
I have forgotten.
But now I see what I am climbing
towards: *Acceptance*
written in capital letters,
a special headline:
Acceptance,
its name in lights.
I struggle on,
waving and shouting.
Below, my whole life spreads its surf,
all the landscapes I've ever known
or dreamed of. Below
a fish jumps: the pulse
in your neck.

Acceptance. I finally
reach it.
But something is wrong.
Grief is a circular staircase.
I have lost you.

—LINDA PASTAN

FROM *Heaven's Coast*

Being in grief, it turns out, is not unlike being in love.

In both states, the imagination's entirely occupied with one person. The beloved dwells at the heart of the world, and becomes a Rome: the roads of feeling all lead to him, all proceed from him. Everything that touches us seems to relate back to that center; there is no other emotional life, no place outside the universe of feeling centered on its pivotal figure.

And in grief, as in love, we're porous, permeable. There is something contagious about this openness. Other people sense it and respond to us differently, since our openness seems to invite them in.

—MARK DOTY

from Rooms Remembered

I needed, for months after he died, to remember our rooms—
     some lit by the trivial, others gentle with an obscurity

that comforted us: it hid our own darkness.
     So for months, duteous, I remembered:

rooms where friends lingered, rooms with our beds,
     with our books, rooms with curtains I sewed

from bright cottons. Tables of laughter,
     a chipped bowl in early light, black

branches by a window, bowing toward night, & those rooms,
     too, in which we came together

to be away from all—& sometimes from ourselves—
     I remembered that, also.

But tonight—as I lean into the doorway to his room
     & stare at dusk settled there—

what I remember best is how, to throw my arms around his neck,
     I needed to stand on the tips of my toes.

—Laure-Anne Bosselaar

In the Same Space

The setting of houses, cafés, the neighborhood
that I've seen and walked through years on end:

I created you while I was happy, while I was sad,
with so many incidents, so many details.

And, for me, the whole of you has been transformed into feeling.

—C. P. CAVAFY

Translated from the Greek by Edmund Keeley and Philip Sherrard

FROM *On My Own*

Throughout this period since John died, I've been trying to define for myself exactly what grief is. The Oxford dictionary has many definitions, including "mental anguish or sorrow...bereavement or bitter regret or remorse." I realize I am in the process of experiencing all of these things. I would add sadness, loneliness, a sense of isolation, self-imposed or otherwise. And, to be honest, some anger, a resentment at having been abandoned.

And what can I do except live through all these things? Continue to put one foot in front of the other. Carry on. Behave normally. Act as though I'm still whole, when a central part of me, which is what John has been for most of my life, is gone.

—DIANE REHM

Naming

If I name this grief,
define it
with guilt
and redemption,
call it drowning,
desolation,
call it
fire and stone,

then I am bound
to care for it,
like a stray cat I name,
that demands I feed him.
He comes and goes,
sometimes demands I feed him.
He comes and goes,
sometimes disappears
for days and then returns,
insisting that
I remember.

—CAROL LYNNE KNIGHT

FROM *The Carry Home*

When something goes wrong out in wild nature—like getting lost—it feels like the world is no longer yours. You've come unmoored in a strange place, in the land of the bear and the wind and the rocks. Jane used to say that as you start searching for clues, as you begin to wander, the trick was to summon the resolve to breathe through that terrifying state of not knowing. Over the years, being in the wild had taught both of us to look such feelings in the eye, to watch them long enough to see clues that might otherwise be buried in panic. Finding a way out never took fierce rationalism. It took the calm courage of attention.

I knew this was also what I needed when wandering through the dark, thorny fields of grief. Being able to muster attention, forgoing the enormous seduction of escape, offers travelers an essential reassurance. In a way it was just a new twist on that old Greek definition of beauty—beauty as "being of one's hour"—even when the path is baffling. Even when you're utterly, completely lost.

—GARY FERGUSON

FROM *Levels of Life*

You ask yourself: to what extent in this turmoil of missing am I missing her, or missing the life we had together, or missing what it was in her that made me more myself, or missing simple companionship, or (not so simple) love, or all or any overlapping bits of each? You ask yourself: what happiness is there in just the memory of happiness? And how in any case might that work, given that happiness has only ever consisted of something shared? Solitary happiness—it sounds like a contradiction in terms, an implausible contraption that will never get off the ground.

—Julian Barnes

FROM *Between Lives*

Dove-gray Paris, most ineffable of cities, was still home base, where there were friends for advice: "*Dorothéa, il faut refaire ta vie*" ("You must remake your life"), meaning *with* someone. Provoking an inward shudder.

　　Spring 1978. A procession of pale afternoons sees me behind the graying curtains of our white rooms. No. I must learn to say "my." My rooms. In the rue de Lille. White all around, of walls and floors turning brownward gray, so mimetic to my mood. Downy goose gray, gentler than all that white. Now the real city is inside, a sift of black that I accept, all defenses down. So in my rooms, where I am polite to all. And where I am instructed as to my situation: not bad, really, if you know your place, do as you're told, do not ask questions, and remember that you are, well, a woman, a widow, and not very reliable. What am I doing here?

—DOROTHEA TANNING

I Am Writing This Blessing

Instead of lying
in bed with him
on this summer afternoon,
I am writing
this blessing.

Instead of watching
how the light falls across us,
I am writing
this blessing.

Instead of tracing
the curve of his back,
I am writing
this blessing.

Instead of placing
my head on his chest,
I am writing
this blessing.

Instead of meeting
his mouth with my mouth,
I am writing
this blessing.

Instead of twining
my legs through his,

I am writing
this blessing.

Instead,
instead,
instead,
I am writing
this blessing still.

—JAN RICHARDSON

The Widow's Lament in Springtime

Sorrow is my own yard
where the new grass
flames as it has flamed
often before but not
with the cold fire
that closes round me this year.
Thirtyfive years
I lived with my husband.
The plumtree is white today
with masses of flowers.
Masses of flowers
load the cherry branches
and color some bushes
yellow and some red
but the grief in my heart
is stronger than they
for though they were my joy
formerly, today I notice them
and turn away forgetting.
Today my son told me
that in the meadows,
at the edge of the heavy woods
in the distance, he saw
trees of white flowers.
I feel that I would like

to go there
and fall into those flowers
and sink into the marsh near them.

—WILLIAM CARLOS WILLIAMS

Summer Solstice

Suddenly,

there's nothing to do

and too much—

the lawn, paths, woods

were never so green

white blossoms of every

size and shape—hydrangea,

Chinese dogwood, mock orange

Spill their glistening—

Inside, your photographs

and books stand guard

in orderly array. Your

half of the bed is smooth,

the pillows plump, the phone

just out of reach beyond it.

No one calls early—they

remember your late hours.

The shades are down, so

sunlight's held at bay

though not the fabulous winged

song of summer birds

waking me as ever, always in our

favorite room, our season.

Yesterday's mail on the desk

newspapers, unread. Plans for the day

hover bright out all our doors—

Don't think of evening.

—Rose Styron

Desideria

Surprised by joy—impatient as the Wind
   I turned to share the transport—O! with whom
   But Thee—deep buried in the silent tomb,
That spot which no vicissitude can find?
Love, faithful love, recall'd thee to my mind—
   But how could I forget thee? Through what power,
   Even for the least division of an hour,
Have I been so beguiled as to be blind
To my most grievous loss?—That thought's return
   Was the worst pang that sorrow ever bore,
Save one, one only, when I stood forlorn,
   Knowing my heart's best treasure was no more;
That neither present time, nor years unborn
   Could to my sight that heavenly face restore.

—WILLIAM WORDSWORTH

I Am Willing

Grief says to me: "You will never love anyone the way you loved Rayya." And I reply: "I am willing for that to be true." Grief says: "She's gone, and she's never coming back." I reply: "I am willing for that to be true." Grief says: "You will never hear that laugh again." I say: "I am willing." Grief says, "You will never smell her skin again." I get down on the floor on my fucking knees, and—and through my sheets of tears—I say, "I AM WILLING." This is the job of the living—to be willing to bow down before EVERY-THING that is bigger than you. And nearly everything in this world is bigger than you.

I don't know where Rayya is now. It's not mine to know. I only know that I will love her forever. And that I am willing.

Onward.

It's an honor to be in grief. It's an honor to feel that much, to have loved that much.

—Elizabeth Gilbert

FROM *A Severe Mercy*

Along with the emptiness, which is what I mean by loss, and along with the grief—loss and grief are not the same thing—I kept wanting to *tell* her about it. We always told each other—that was what sharing was—and now this huge thing was happening to me, and I couldn't tell her. Someone speaking of the pain of stopping smoking remarked: If only I could have a cigarette while I suffer! I sometimes thought I could bear the loss and grief if only I could tell her about it. So I did. I wrote to her in the quiet evenings—I did not go out at all—and told her. Writing a letter is a real form of conversation in which the image of a distant person is held in one's mind. I could not have spoken aloud to thin air with any sense of reality, nor could I now write to her, but then I could really speak to her in letters. I did not save them or reread them, those long letters of our companionship, but I could write them—to her. Whether she read them, over my shoulder perhaps, is of course a different matter.

—SHELDON VANAUKEN

Long Distance II

Though my mother was already two years dead
Dad kept her slippers warming by the gas,
put hot water bottles her side of the bed
and still went to renew her transport pass.

You couldn't just drop in. You had to phone.
He'd put you off an hour to give him time
to clear away her things and look alone
as though his still raw love were such a crime.

He couldn't risk my blight of disbelief
though sure that very soon he'd hear her key
scrape in the rusted lock and end his grief.
He knew she'd just popped out to get the tea.

I believe life ends with death, and that is all.
You haven't both gone shopping; just the same,
in my new black leather phone book there's your name
and the disconnected number I still call.

—Tony Harrison

The Embrace

You weren't well or really ill yet either;
just a little tired, your handsomeness
tinged by grief or anticipation, which brought
to your face a thoughtful, deepening grace.

I didn't for a moment doubt you were dead.
I knew that to be true still, even in the dream.
You'd been out—at work maybe?—
having a good day, almost energetic.

We seemed to be moving from some old house
where we'd lived, boxes everywhere, things
in disarray: that was the *story* of my dream,
but even asleep I was shocked out of the narrative

by your face, the physical fact of your face:
inches from mine, smooth shaven, loving, alert.
Why so difficult, remembering the actual look
of you? Without a photograph, without strain?

So when I saw your unguarded, reliable face,
your unmistakable gaze opening all the warmth
and clarity of —warm brown tea—we held
each other for the time the dream allowed.

Bless you. You came back, so I could see you
once more, plainly, so I could rest against you
without thinking this happiness lessened anything,
without thinking you were alive again.

—MARK DOTY

FROM *Blue Peninsula*

What exactly was so unappealing to me about the terms *grief management* and *grief work*? Granted, difficult, complex things demand management and work. I suspected formulaic advice, and my energy for potentially disappointing directions was limited. When I browsed through "how to grieve" books and "basic grief skills" manuals, they left me alone, delivered nothing that stayed. Grief has weight. Much of the writing about "handling" it did not. There were too many stepladders of the stages of grief, framed by quotes and butterflies and flowers, and there was not enough poetry. No rancid rage, no bitter phrases, no companions in my choking despair, no depth and breadth to keep me company in my sorrow's labyrinths. Too much in these books was antiseptic and distancing and sometimes moving too quickly to the light, the redemption, the blessing in the pain. "Says *who*?" I cried or screamed at different times.

—MADGE MCKEITHEN

Talking to Grief

Ah, Grief, I should not treat you
like a homeless dog
who comes to the back door
for a crust, for a meatless bone.
I should trust you.

I should coax you
into the house and give you
your own corner,
a worn mat to lie on,
your own water dish.

You think I don't know you've been living
under my porch.
You long for your real place to be readied
before winter comes. You need
your name,
your collar and tag. You need
the right to warn off intruders,
to consider
my house your own
and me your person
and yourself
my own dog.

—DENISE LEVERTOV

FROM *First Comes Love*

A couple of months after Tony died, I was driving the kids to school and "Modern Love" came on the radio, the old David Bowie song that was so popular the year we met. As has become almost inevitable when I listen to the radio, I started crying— whole decades of popular music do this to me now. Commercials do this to me, cemeteries, beauty salons, getting a massage, not getting a massage, tall, thin men, men with wire-rimmed glasses, billboards for Newport 100s, waking up in the middle of the night, trying to pick a movie to rent, the list goes on.

Vincie, already familiar with the phenomenon, asked, Does this song remind you of Daddy?

Yes, I told him, this was one of our favorite songs.

Don't you think it's still one of his favorite songs? asked Vince.

Oh, Vincie, I don't know, I answered, holding back a sob of frustration. I don't even know if they have music in heaven.

Well, why don't we open the windows? he suggested.

Do what?

Open the windows, so Daddy can hear it in heaven.

—MARION WINIK

The Well of Grief

Those who will not slip beneath
    the still surface on the well of grief,

turning down through its black water
    to the place we cannot breathe,

will never know the source from which we drink,
    the secret water, cold and clear,

nor find in the darkness glimmering,
    the small round coins,
        thrown by those who wished for something else.

—DAVID WHYTE

Saudade

means nostalgia, I'm told, but also
nostalgia for what never was. Isn't it
the same thing? At a café
in Rio flies wreathe my glass.

How you would have loved this: the waiter
sweating his knit shirt dark. Children
loping, in tiny suits or long shorts, dragging
toys and towels to the beach. We talk,

or I talk, and imagine your answer, the heat clouding our view.
Here, again, grief fashioned in its cruelest translation:
my imagined you is all I have left of you.

—JOHN FREEMAN

Separation

Your absence has gone through me
Like thread through a needle.
Everything I do is stitched with its color.

—W. S. Merwin

Absolutely Clear

Don't surrender your loneliness
So quickly.
Let it cut more deep.

Let it ferment and season you
As few human
Or even divine ingredients can.

Something missing in my heart tonight
Has made my eyes so soft,
My voice
So tender,

My need of God
Absolutely
Clear.

—HAFIZ

Translated from the Persian by Daniel Ladinsky

Benediction

God banish from your house
The fly, the roach, the mouse

That riots in the walls
Until the plaster falls;

Admonish from your door
The hypocrite and liar;

No shy, soft, tigrish fear
Permit upon your stair,

Nor agents of your doubt.
God drive them whistling out.

Let nothing touched with evil,
Let nothing that can shrivel

Heart's tenderest frond, intrude
Upon your still, deep blood.

Against the drip of night
God keep all windows tight,

Protect your mirrors from
Surprise, delirium,

Admit no trailing wind
Into your shuttered mind

To plume the lake of sleep
With dreams. If you must weep

God give you tears, but leave
You secrecy to grieve,

And islands for your pride,
And love to nest in your side.

—Stanley Kunitz

FROM Try to Praise the Mutilated World

Remember the moments when we were together
in a white room and the curtain fluttered.
Return in thought to the concert where music flared.
You gathered acorns in the park in autumn
and leaves eddied over the earth's scars.
Praise the mutilated world
and the gray feather a thrush lost,
and the gentle light that strays and vanishes
and returns.

—ADAM ZAGAJEWSKI

Translated from the Polish by Clare Cavanagh

Work-Clothes Quilt

With nothing but time
and the light of the Singer,
and no one to come now forever

and rattle the bell
at the backdoor and scatter
black mud on the stoop,
and make that small moan
as he heaves off his boots—

with no one to fill
the big kettle and set it,
and fall asleep talking
to the back of her neck
as the treadle-belt hums—

with nobody, nowhere
in need of such things,
she unbuckles his belt
for the last time

and cuts up his pant legs
and rips out the double-stitched seams,
making patches of plackets
and oil-stained pockets,
of kerchiefs, and collars, and sleeves,

her fingers setting the bobbin
and clamping the foot
until she's joined every scrap she can salvage,

no matter how brown
with his sweat,
or stiff with his blisters,
or blooming his roses
of pine-tar, and gear-grease, and blood—

   until,

as the wedding clock chimes
and his buried bones freeze,
as frost gleams
at sunrise in the window,

she stands by the bed
and breathes his dark scent

then wraps herself
in it and sleeps.

—Patrick Phillips

Trying to Raise the Dead

Look at me. I'm standing on a deck
in the middle of Oregon. There are
people inside the house. It's not my

house, you don't know them.
They're drinking and singing
and playing guitars. You love

this song. Remember? "Ophelia."
Boards on the windows, mail
by the door. I'm whispering

so they won't think I'm crazy.
They don't know me that well.
Where are you now? I feel stupid.

I'm talking to trees, to leaves
swarming on the black air, stars
blinking in and out of heart-

shaped shadows, to the moon, half-
lit and barren, stuck like an ax
between the branches. What are you

now? Air? Mist? Dust? Light?
What? Give me something. I have
to know where to send my voice.

A direction. An object. My love, it needs
a place to rest. Say anything. I'm listening.
I'm ready to believe. Even lies, I don't care.

Say, burning bush. Say, stone. They've
stopped singing now and I really should go.
So tell me, quickly. It's April. I'm

on Spring Street. That's my gray car
in the driveway. They're laughing
and dancing. Someone's bound

to show up soon. I'm waving.
Give me a sign if you can see me.
I'm the only one here on my knees.

—DORIANNE LAUX

FROM *Strange Paradise*

For me there is no letting go. Details call for attention. His wishes will have to be carried out. In the fall I'll go to the concerts on the tickets Jerry ordered knowing he probably wouldn't live until then. Seven pairs of them attest to the power of his wish to live. Until then, resolved to do everyday tasks, I'll go through a normal morning when suddenly grief arrives in a high whitecap wave: after another lull, the comber rises and flattens me. Still, I find in the breaker's aftermath a place for the work that clarifies. Into the northeaster at sea a dinghy comes, splintered, in need of repair. I climb aboard and try to bail it out. I go on.

—GRACE SCHULMAN

A letter to Grace Schulman

Alas, I know about those "waves"—and how they up-end you, spin you in the breaker-line—just when you thought you might be getting back on your feet, standing upright. But they do recede, don't they? And then there are the skimmers and terns and the real bay and the music.

I'm not sure that wished-for things are ever believable—that "love is as strong as death." But we must believe something is unceasing, in order to go on with our lives. I will never celebrate death—it is cruel and indiscriminate—it crushes children and youth and cripples and annihilates the old. Yet it cannot entirely erase us. And I know that our relationships with the dead go on—and on. Perhaps they deepen—certainly they are filled with new pained wonder in the altered presences of the lost.

—CAROL MUSKE-DUKES
From Strange Paradise *by Grace Schulman*

In the Garden

St Francis in Frank Caswell's garden stands
watch over hostas and daylilies and
Frank's dead wife's cremated remains, planted

years back after ovarian cancer
had had its miserable way with her.
He was a young man then. She was younger.

He clenched his teeth and had her body burned
and paid the bill and hustled back to work
like nothing had happened; like the stone bird

on the still shoulder of her garden saint
which never flew or sang but still remained
solid and silent and ever vigilant

through the slow seasons of his bereavement.
One June for no particular reason
he took the ashes out and scattered them

among her overgrown perennials.
And once the trees were pruned and weeds were pulled,
the bird-bath and all the bird feeders filled,

Frank sat alone and wept inconsolably
and prayed to be an instrument of peace
and wondered if only a saint or a sissy

or someone crazy with the loss of love
would labor so to keep something alive?
One day he swore he saw the statue move.

—Thomas Lynch

FROM *The Light of the World*

I feel certain I can wait forever for him to come back. I leave the light on in the living room, the light that faces the street. If I am patient he will come back. If I sit on the stoop through the night he will come at dawn. He would have waited forever for me; he never was not there waiting for me. I can wait and wait and wait, as long as it takes.

Gone on a trip? Hiding in the crawl space under the stairs? Visiting a sick relative? Around the corner, picking up milk and eggs? Sitting in a café lost in an esoteric book?

I will wait for as long as it takes for him to return to me. He will return to find the children grown tall, perhaps married, perhaps with children named for him. He will return to find me composed in my starched dress and head-bonnet, waiting in the same wood-framed domicile he'd left.

Last night I thought he came on a skateboard in my dream, but of course, it was not him. He turned and smiled to me and was someone else, and skated away.

I am getting older and he is not.

—ELIZABETH ALEXANDER

FROM Redemption Song

...Grief might be easy
if there wasn't still
such beauty—would be far
simpler if the silver

maple didn't thrust
its leaves into flame,
trusting that spring
will find it again.

All this might be easier if
there wasn't a song
still lifting us above it,
if wind didn't trouble

my mind like water.
I half expect to see you
fill the autumn air
like breath—

At night I sleep
on clenched fists.
Days I'm like the child
who on the playground

falls, crying
not so much from pain

as surprise.
I'm tired of tide

taking you away,
then back again—
what's worse, the forgetting
or the thing

you can't forget.
Neither yet—
last summer's
choir of crickets

grown quiet.

—KEVIN YOUNG

FROM *Levels of Life*

Grief-work. It sounds such a clear and solid concept, with its confident two-part name. But it is fluid, slippery, metamorphic. Sometimes it is passive, a waiting for time and pain to disappear; sometimes active, a conscious attention to death and loss and the loved one; sometimes necessarily distractive (the bland football match, the overwhelming opera). And you have never done this kind of work before. It is unpaid and yet not voluntary; it is rigorous, yet there is no overseer; it is skilled, yet there is no apprenticeship. And it is hard to tell whether you are making progress; or what would help you do so. Theme song for youth (sung by the Supremes): "You Can't Hurry Love." Theme song for age (arranged for any instrument): "You Can't Hurry Grief."

—JULIAN BARNES

Gone / Away

Gone or away? Right now I prefer away
because a storm rolls down through the valley
with its load of leaves, twigs, bird nests
and soil from another continent
and makes the windows on the sunroom rattle like a castle in
    Siberia.
Saying gone would resonate too deeply
and damage the foundations of the house.
Away is a small white cloud, a kite
in a bleak September sky
a wheelbarrow tipped over on the edge of the woods
a striped sock on the riverbank
away is the white pebbles on the bottom of a brook
whose water knows the secrets of astronomy.
With the changing seasons I have thought of you
as a wanderer between gone and away
a homeless soul, an eye that cannot shut.
As fast as fire, water, darkness, and sun overtake each other
on this afternoon early in January
I can only think of you as gone away. With the emphasis on
    gone.

—HENRIK NORDBRANDT
Translated from the Danish by Thom Satterlee

FROM *Two-Part Invention*

But grief still has to be worked through. It is like walking through water. Sometimes there are little waves lapping about my feet. Sometimes there is an enormous breaker that knocks me down. Sometimes there is a sudden and fierce squall. But I know that many waters cannot quench love, neither can the floods drown it.

We are not good about admitting grief, we Americans. It is embarrassing. We turn away, afraid that it might happen to us....

Does a marriage end with the death of one of the partners? In a way, yes. I made my promises to Hugh "till death do us part," and that has happened. But the marriage contract is not the love that builds up over many years, and which never ends, as the circle of our wedding band never ends. Hugh will always be part of me, go with me wherever I go, and that is good because, despite our faults and flaws and failures, what we gave each other was good. I am who I am because of our years together, freed by his acceptance and love of me.

—MADELEINE L'ENGLE

Vigil

Why not wake at dawn? Why not break
From the coffin of night, whose nails
Are the only stars left. Why not follow
A tear like a comet's tail, and trail
The grief of a year until it ends—
Who knows where. Why not wake
At dawn, after all is gone, and go on?

—PHILLIS LEVIN

from *No Longer Than a Sigh*

I must admit that for the first time memories invade me. I call them up, I ask their help to live. I come back to myself and forage in the past. Sometimes I resent you for being dead. You have deserted me, left me....

I no longer look for your face. For a long time you sprang up everywhere. How to find a path, a street, a quay that we haven't explored together? I had either to flee or to brave all these places alone. In the many faces of the crowd or in the solitude of a woodland path I saw nothing but your face. My reason refused these mirages, but my heart searched them out. You were both absent and present. Every hour I questioned myself: how is it possible that I live—not that I live, but simply that my heart continued to beat now that yours has stopped? I sometimes heard it said that you are present among us. I agreed. What good would it do to deny it? I told myself that it is easy for some to accept death. Are they trying to reassure themselves of their own eternity?

—ANNE PHILIPE
Translated from the French by Cornelia Schaeffer

FROM *Here If You Need Me*

When it comes to music and mourning, stick to instrumentals. Songs with words are booby traps. You think you're okay, then some sweet-voiced crooner starts singing of loss in a minor key, and you aren't just leaking water from your eyes, you are down on the floor and grief is a splintery thing the size of a telephone pole, shoving its way through your chest. My advice: listen to classical music, preferably baroque.

Alanis Morissette, bless her heart, had recently released an album called *Jagged Little Pill*, and the children and I used to listen to it over and over while we drove to and from preschool and swimming lessons and karate.

We would sing along: "I feel drunk but I'm sober...I'm brave but I'm chickenshit."...

Alanis was safe for me to listen to because all her songs were angry. The sole stage in Elisabeth Kübler-Ross's stages of grief that I seemed to be skipping was the anger stage, because there was no one to be angry with. Drew's death was an accident. No one intended it: not the speeder he was turning to go after, not the driver of the truck, not Drew himself, God knows. So I wasn't angry. It hurt. That's all.

—KATE BRAESTRUP

FROM *A Grief Observed*

It is hard to have patience with people who say, "There is no death" or "Death doesn't matter." There is death. And whatever is matters. And whatever happens has consequences, and it and they are irrevocable and irreversible. You might as well say that birth doesn't matter. I look up at the night sky. Is anything more certain than that in all those vast times and spaces, if I were allowed to search them, I should nowhere find her face, her voice, her touch? She died. She is dead. Is the word so difficult to learn?

—C. S. Lewis

FROM *Nothing Was the Same*

I learned to live in expectation of assault. From nowhere, a memory of Richard would compel me, like some recollected scent, into a region of my mind whose existence I had forgotten. Then I would coil to protect myself, huddle as prey against predator. *He cannot be gone*, I would rail against the gods, caught again in the presence of his absence. *He will not be back*, I would know after each new confrontation. It became clearer over time, less wavering. *He will not be back. He has been away too long.*

—KAY REDFIELD JAMISON

Lost

Stand still. The trees ahead and bushes beside you
Are not lost. Wherever you are is called Here,
And you must treat it as a powerful stranger,
Must ask permission to know it and be known.
The forest breathes. Listen. It answers,
I have made this place around you.
If you leave it, you may come back again, saying Here.
No two trees are the same to Raven.
No two branches are the same to Wren.
If what a tree or a bush does is lost on you,
You are surely lost. Stand still. The forest knows
Where you are. You must let it find you.

—David Wagoner

Michiko Dead

He manages like somebody carrying a box
that is too heavy, first with his arms
underneath. When their strength gives out,
he moves the hands forward, hooking them
on the corners, pulling the weight against
his chest. He moves his thumbs slightly
when the fingers begin to tire, and it makes
different muscles take over. Afterward,
he carries it on his shoulder, until the blood
drains out of the arm that is stretched up
to steady the box and the arm goes numb. But now
the man can hold underneath again, so that
he can go on without ever putting the box down.

—JACK GILBERT

Heavy

That time
I thought I could not
go any closer to grief
without dying

I went closer,
and I did not die.
Surely God
had His hand in this,

as well as friends.
Still, I was bent,
and my laughter,
as the poet said,

was nowhere to be found.
Then said my friend Daniel
(brave even among lions),
"It's not the weight you carry

but how you carry it—
books, bricks, grief—
it's all in the way
you embrace it, balance it, carry it

when you cannot, and would not,
put it down."

So I went practicing.
Have you noticed?

Have you heard
the laughter
that comes, now and again,
out of my startled mouth?

How I linger
to admire, admire, admire
the things of this world
that are kind, and maybe

also troubled—
roses in the wind,
the sea geese on the steep waves,
a love
to which there is no reply?

—MARY OLIVER

PART III

Turning

FROM *M Train*

And slowly the leaves of my life turned, and I saw myself pointing out simple things to Fred, *skies of blue, clouds of white*, hoping to penetrate the veil of a congenital sorrow. I saw his pale eyes looking intently into mine, trying to trap my walleye in his unfaltering gaze. That alone took up several pages that filled me with such painful longing that I fed them into the fire in my heart, like Gogol burning page by page the manuscript of *Dead Souls Two*. I burned them all, one by one; they did not form ash, did not go cold, but radiated the warmth of human compassion.

—PATTI SMITH

The Window

Your body is away from me,
But there is a window open
From my Heart to Yours.
From this window, like the moon,
I keep sending news secretly to You.

—RUMI

Translated from the Persian by Nevit Oguz Ergin

FROM *Sparrow*

The words and phrases that have bubbled up to the surface the past months—I think these are part of the vocabulary that's been taking shape, without my quite knowing at the time: *Listen. Ask. Receive. You must be very still.*

I also had a sense, very early on, of God or you wanting me to know: *You have all the time in the world to go a little crazy.*

—JAN RICHARDSON

A Different Sun

Silent around the boat, silent
like stars when Earth is switched off and people's words,
faltering thoughts and dreams are forgotten.
I place the oars in their rowlocks,
lower and raise them. Listen.
The small splash of drops in the ocean
cement the silence. Slowly, towards a different sun
I turn my boat in the mist: The tight-knit nothing
of life. And row,
row.

—KOLBEIN FALKEID
Translated from the Norwegian

FROM Grace

On the lawn of memory,
        violets suddenly appear: each a sensation

like a note, but without the dirge of loss,
        translucent, welcome, unexpected.

Photo albums open their leaves
        with a calm that seems phenomenal.

Tonight the sun reclines in the sky,
        and time is a kneeling animal.

—DIANE ACKERMAN

Dream

You're alive and riding your bicycle
to school and I am worried about you
riding your bicycle all the way to school
so I get in my car and drive like a maniac
through the dream over curbs and lawns
sideswiping statuary and birdbaths along
the way frantically seeking you everywhere
the rear wheel of your bicycle disappearing
around the next corner and the next and then
I am riding a bicycle too and sounding
the alarm which sounds like a bicycle bell
so no one believes it's an alarm and I pedal
faster and faster my knees bumping up against
the handlebars which by now have sprouted
ribbons with pompoms and a basket attached
with your lunch inside and I'm pedaling to save
my life and your life and finally when I find you
in the dream you aren't dead yet you're alive
and a little angry and embarrassed to see me
all out of breath on a girl's bicycle holding
your lunch out in my hand trembling with joy

—Paul Hostovsky

FROM *Because What Else Could I Do*

On the evening of the six-month day I drove

into the hills a rivered town a little café to read

my poems to strangers and friends and at

the end I read *go with me   into that night where one*

will go before   read *moon by night*   read *night*

night my love   by and by   and there

was silence because (they told me after) when I

read *go* the door opened but no one was there

and when I read   *by*   the door closed

—Martha Collins

FROM The River

Grief's crater in the landscape of the present grows smaller and smaller. Some days, though, I itch to claw the crater deeper. This is the hole that love left, and some part of me craves the ache of fresh dirt, the raw scar, the pain that feels like a heart attack. I hunger for news of the dead, and lately, no one's come to visit me.

—DENISE EMANUEL CLEMEN

FROM *Nothing Was the Same*

Grief taught through indirection. It was an unyielding teacher, shrewd and brutal. It attacked, soft and insidious at times, gale force at others, insistent that I see Richard from first one slant and then another—sometimes in fragments, at others full-on—until I could put him, and the two of us as we had been together, in the more distant place where all to do with him had to be. Memory and regret bypassed my rational mind and saw themselves straight into the festering places.

I fought hard against this, defiant. *If he cannot stay*, I would rail at Grief, *do not bring him back*. But grief teaches in its own way, and thoughts of Richard came and went in a manner not of my choosing. Grief, pre-Adamic and excellently evolved, knew how best to do what it had to do. Richard had to come and go, return and leave again, if he was to take leave in the way he must. He had to take leave in order that I might find a new place for him; in order that I might find a new way to be with him, in order for life to go on. Or so I found some peace in believing.

—KAY REDFIELD JAMISON

FROM For Daphne at Lone Lake

Speak of your heart
burned to a seed of ash,
and love, a small white stone
gleaming in the shallows.

—JOHN HAINES

FROM *The Year of Magical Thinking*

The craziness is receding but no clarity is taking its place.

I look for resolution and find none.

I do not want to finish the year because I know that as the days pass, as January becomes February and February becomes summer, certain things will happen. My image of John at the instant of his death will become less immediate, less raw. It will become something that happened in another year. My sense of John himself, John alive, will become more remote, even "mudgy," softened, transmuted into whatever best serves my life without him. In fact this is already beginning to happen. All year I have been keeping time by last year's calendar: what were we doing on this day last year, where did we have dinner, is it the day a year ago we flew to Honolulu after Quintana's wedding, is it the day a year ago we flew back from Paris, *is it the day*. I realized today for the first time that my memory of this day a year ago is a memory that does not involve John....

I know why we try to keep the dead alive: we try to keep them alive in order to keep them with us.

I also know that if we are to live ourselves there comes a point at which we must relinquish the dead, let them go, keep them dead.

Let them become the photograph on the table.

Let them become the name on the trust accounts.

Let go of them in the water.

—JOAN DIDION

FROM Washing the Elephant

And though dailiness may have no place
for the ones that have etched themselves in the laugh lines
and frown lines on the face that's harder and harder
to claim as your own, often one love-of-your-life
will appear in a dream, arriving
with the weight and certitude of an elephant,
and it's always the heart that wants to go out and wash
the huge mysteriousness of what they meant, those memories
that have only memories to feed them, and only you to keep
    them clean.

—Barbara Ras

FROM *Safekeeping*

She thinks of his dying as a hole he fell through, a hole in the day that opened and then closed back over him. But he is still here; she feels him near. She feels him all the time. She assumes he knows now, everything she meant to say. She hopes so anyway.

Once they walked down Broadway and passed the church on 114th whose message board often quoted Woody Allen (90 PER-CENT OF LIFE IS JUST SHOWING UP), but on that particular day it was blank. "Look," he'd said, surprise in his voice, "the Presbyterians have run out of things to say." He put his arm around her shoulders (he was still able to walk then). "You appreciate me," he'd said then. But maybe you had to be there. She had been there; he had been there; they had been there together.

—ABIGAIL THOMAS

FROM Rooms Remembered

Then, you stop weeping. Lift your face from your hands.
      Not because you're done or because it helped,
            but because there's a faint knock at the window.

You look up. It's a branch. It taps & waves & distracts
      your sorrow. You wipe your face
            hard with both hands.

This is not a sign. You're ruefully aware of that, & don't
      believe in signs. They announced a storm,
            it nears. That's all.

Yet the sky is so still—so lit. Again, those knocks
      at the window. It's not him.
            Of course it isn't.

—LAURE-ANNE BOSSELAAR

FROM *The Best of Us*

I put the key in the lock. Stepped in the door. Breathed in the smell of an old summer cottage. Through the windows, late afternoon sun streamed in. I could see the water dappling in the places where the trout came up to feed.

"How Jim would have loved this," I said. If he were here with me, he'd light a cigar on the porch and rest his feet on the railing. He'd watch as I walked down to the water, and he would keep his eyes on me until I reached the shore again. My guard dog.

And after, over a good meal, we'd have many things to tell each other. What happens to those things, I asked myself, when there is no longer anyone to tell?

It was just me now—a woman with her laptop, wearing a blue-and-white-checked flannel shirt to keep her warm on chilly nights, looking up at the constellations whose names she tries to remember and sometimes does, though from this hemisphere the Magellanic Cloud was not in evidence.

One solitary woman and one solitary loon. Every night that summer, from where I slept in the boathouse down by the water, I heard his long, mournful cry. Somewhere out there at the other side of the shore maybe, her mate would call out to her. Every morning, just as the sun came up, I'd stand at the water's edge for a moment. Then swim.

—JOYCE MAYNARD

Alone

I never thought Michiko would come back
after she died. But if she did, I knew
it would be as a lady in a long white dress.
It is strange that she has returned
as somebody's dalmatian. I meet
the man walking her on a leash
almost every week. He says good morning
and I stoop down to calm her. He said
once that she was never like that with
other people. Sometimes she is tethered
on their lawn when I go by. If nobody
is around, I sit on the grass. When she
finally quiets, she puts her head in my lap
and we watch each other's eyes as I whisper
in her soft ears. She cares nothing about
the mystery. She likes it best when
I touch her head and tell her small
things about my days and our friends.
That makes her happy the way it always did.

—JACK GILBERT

FROM *A Widow's Story*

August 11, 2008. Last night the garden was suffused with light—a strange sort of sourceless sunshine that seemed to come from all directions. I could not see clearly but the garden seemed both my garden—ours—Ray's and mine—and a larger, less cultivated setting. And Ray was—somewhere?—Ray was close by—Ray was turned to me, though I could not see his face clearly—and I felt such relief, saying *You're all right, then. You're here.*

—JOYCE CAROL OATES

What the Living Do

Johnny, the kitchen sink has been clogged for days, some utensil
   probably fell down there.
And the Drano won't work but smells dangerous, and the crusty
   dishes have piled up

waiting for the plumber I still haven't called. This is the everyday
   we spoke of.
It's winter again: the sky's a deep, headstrong blue, and the
   sunlight pours through

the open living-room windows because the heat's on too high in
   here and I can't turn it off.
For weeks now, driving, or dropping a bag of groceries in the
   street, the bag breaking,

I've been thinking: This is what the living do. And yesterday,
   hurrying along those
wobbly bricks in the Cambridge sidewalk, spilling my coffee
   down my wrist and sleeve,

I thought it again, and again later, when buying a hairbrush: This
   is it.
Parking. Slamming the car door shut in the cold. What you called
   that yearning.

What you finally gave up. We want the spring to come and the
   winter to pass. We want

whoever to call or not call, a letter, a kiss—we want more and
        more and then more of it.

But there are moments, walking, when I catch a glimpse
        of myself in the window glass,
say, the window of the corner video store, and I'm gripped by a
        cherishing so deep

for my own blowing hair, chapped face, and unbuttoned coat that
        I'm speechless:
I am living. I remember you.

—MARIE HOWE

FROM *Geography of the Heart*

I am standing on the hill above the apartment where I now live, where I have lived alone since Larry died. The bright white bowl of the city spreads out below. To the north the copper-red towers of the Golden Gate Bridge rise against the tawny Marin headlands.

I am in California, not in France. It is years later, I am here and he is not but love goes on, this is the lesson that I have taken, for a comfort that must and will suffice. In grief there is renewal, of love and so of life.

—FENTON JOHNSON

the raising of lazarus

the dead shall rise again
whoever say
dust must be dust
don't see the trees
smell rain
remember africa
everything that goes
can come
stand up
even the dead shall rise

—LUCILLE CLIFTON

FROM A Change of Plan

What the dead don't know piles up, though we don't notice it at first. They don't know how we're getting along without them, of course, dealing with the hours and days that now accrue so quickly, and, unless they divined this somehow in advance, they don't know that we don't want this inexorable onslaught of breakfasts and phone calls and going to the bank, all this stepping along, because we don't want anything extraneous to get in the way of what we feel about them or the ways we want to hold them in mind. But they're in a hurry, too, or so it seems. Because nothing is happening with them, they are flying away, over that wall, while we are still chained and handcuffed to the weather and the iPhone, to the hurricane and the election and to the couple that's recently moved in downstairs, in Apartment 2-S, with a young daughter and a new baby girl, and we're flying off in the opposite direction at a million miles an hour. It would take many days now, just to fill Carol in.

—ROGER ANGELL

FROM A Widow's First Five Years

My shoulders felt lighter. Space opened within me like a window with the first spring cleaning. There was just enough room for the vestiges of grief to escape.

How can this be? I've wondered. This slow easing of grief is as mundane and astounding as a miracle. And like all miracles, it happens every day. The world is full of sorrow and the end of sorrow. Who would believe such a thing?

—Barbara Lazear Ascher

Heaven

It will be the past
And we'll live there together.

Not as it was *to live*
but as it is remembered.

It will be the past.
We'll all go back together.

Everyone we ever loved,
and lost, and must remember.

It will be the past.
And it will last forever.

—Patrick Phillips

FROM *The Carry Home*

Since Jane's death I'd been swimming against a noxious sense of betrayal. As if the wilds had done me wrong. Not that we both didn't fully understand the risk of being in the outback. We'd canoed together for twenty years....Still, having always been fed by the wilds, encouraged by them even on brutal days, it was incredibly hard to think of them as the stage for her death.

The change came utterly without effort, while sitting on a stump outside my house near the swing I'd made for her, under a canopy of autumn leaves. At one point my eyes came to rest on a dying old cottonwood tree on the other side of the creek. And in that moment, I began surrendering to the inevitability of the end of things. To the fact that not one of the trees in front of me, not the grasses underfoot or the chickadees flitting through the aspen, not the ravens circling overhead, could've arisen in the world without being tied to that same conclusion....

Grace seems to show itself more readily in the wake of grief, slipping into the room like a late-arriving lover and easing between the sheets. Who knows, maybe paying such close attention during the first scattering of Jane's ashes, mustering the focus it seemed to require, left me somehow ready for grace, better able to grasp some essential sliver of understanding. All I can say is, in what proved the first easy thing since the accident, I got off that stump and walked back to the house and through the kitchen door. And never again did I think of nature betraying me.

—GARY FERGUSON

FROM To a Woman Now Dead

A sparrow tapping against my window awakens me at dawn—
    as you used to
And the gloxinia flowers on my nightstand quietly blossom—
    as you used to

Awakening all of my senses, the morning breeze arrives like a
    woman
It's five in the morning, and my bedroom is cool with your
    fragrance

Kicking off the white sheets, I stretch my arms
In the summer sunshine, I imagine your smile

You are still here—right here
You have become all things and I am full of you

Although I am not worthy of it
Your love enfolds me unendingly

—KŌTARŌ TAKAMURA

Translated from the Japanese by Leanne Ogasawara

Slice of Moon

There's a slice of moon
left over in the sky, a sliver
of carnival glass wedged

into the milky blue,
as if the Gods
had a midnight party,

couldn't finish it all,
left a piece of moon
for us, barely throbbing

in the morning light,
a crescent of white
hanging onto the sober sky.

Why is it still up there
on this new day?
Its job, to taunt darkness,

burn through the night
like heaven's candle,
igniting our dreams,

should be over. Why
does this moon persist?
The sun sets as it's meant to,

leaves the sky gracefully,
falling into the arms
of the ocean.

We can trust it to disappear
so the sky can darken,
so we may rest, rocked

by the pale memory
of motion, rocked by the song
our lover sang or never sang.

—KIM DOWER

Birdwings

Your grief for what you've lost lifts a mirror
up to where you're bravely working.

Expecting the worst, you look, and instead
here's the joyful face you've been wanting to see.

Your hand opens and closes and opens and closes.
If it were always a fist or always stretched open,
you would be paralyzed.

Your deepest presence is in every small contracting
                                    and expanding,
the two as beautifully balanced and coordinated
as birdwings.

—RUMI

Translated from the Persian by Coleman Barks with John Moyne

Eagle Poem

To pray you open your whole self
To sky, to earth, to sun, to moon
To one whole voice that is you.
And know there is more
That you can't see, can't hear;
Can't know except in moments
Steadily growing, and in languages
That aren't always sound but other
Circles of motion.
Like eagle that Sunday morning
Over Salt River. Circled in blue sky
In wind, swept our hearts clean
With sacred wings.
We see you, see ourselves and know
That we must take the utmost care
And kindness in all things.
Breathe in, knowing we are made of
All this, and breathe, knowing
We are truly blessed because we
Were born, and die soon within a
True circle of motion,
Like eagle rounding out the morning
Inside us.
We pray that it will be done
In beauty.
In beauty.

—JOY HARJO

Yes

Now we are like that flat cone of sand
in the garden of the Silver Pavilion in Kyōto
designed to appear only in moonlight.

Do you want me to mourn?
Do you want me to wear black?

Or like moonlight on whitest sand
To use your dark, to gleam, to shimmer?

I gleam.   I mourn.

—TESS GALLAGHER

The temple bell stops

The temple bell stops.
But the sound keeps coming
out of the flowers.

—BASHŌ

Translated from the Japanese by Robert Bly

Twice Blessed

So that I stopped
there
and looked
into the waters
seeing not only
my reflected face
but the great sky
that framed
my lonely figure
and after a moment
I lifted my hands
and then my eyes
and I allowed myself
to be astonished
by the great
everywhere
calling to me
like an old
and unspoken
invitation,
made new
by the sun
and the spring,
and the cloud
and the light,
like something
both
calling to me

and radiating
from where I stood,
as if I could
understand
everything
I had been given
and everything ever
taken from me,
as if I could be
everything I have ever
learned
and everything
I could ever know,
as if I knew
both the way I had come
and, secretly,
the way
underneath
I was still
promised to go,
brought together,
like this, with the
unyielding ground
and the symmetry
of the moving sky,
caught in still waters.

Someone I have been,
and someone
I am just,

about to become,
something I am
and will be forever,
the sheer generosity
of being loved
through loving:
the miracle reflection
of a twice blessed life.

—David Whyte

love is a place

love is a place
& through this place of
love move
(with brightness of peace)
all places

yes is a world
& in this world of
yes live
(skillfully curled)
all worlds

—E.E. CUMMINGS

In Blackwater Woods

Look, the trees
are turning
their own bodies
into pillars

of light,
are giving off the rich
fragrance of cinnamon
and fulfillment,

the long tapers
of cattails
are bursting and floating away over
the blue shoulders

of the ponds,
and every pond,
no matter what its
name is, is

nameless now.
Every year
everything
I have ever learned

in my lifetime
leads back to this: the fires

and the black river of loss
whose other side

is salvation,
whose meaning
none of us will ever know.
To live in this world

you must be able
to do three things:
to love what is mortal;
to hold it

against your bones knowing
your own life depends on it;
and, when the time comes to let it go,
to let it go.

—MARY OLIVER

Acknowledgments

With thanks and gratitude—

to the writers and poets I've quoted;
to the friends who read early drafts, especially Sally Court and
    Paula Diamond;
to my agent, Lisa Erbach Vance, everyone at the Aaron M. Priest
    Literary Agency, and always Aaron and Arleen;
to my editor Jason Gardner and copy editor Kristen Cashman
    at New World Library, and also designer and typesetter Tona
    Pearce Myers, cover designer Vicki Kuskowski, publicist Tristy
    Taylor, and Marketing Director Munro Magruder;
and to Joe Morgenstern.

Permission Acknowledgments

Every effort has been made to trace the ownership of all copyrighted material included in this volume and to secure the necessary permissions to reprint these selections. In the event of any question arising as to the use of any material, the editor and the publisher, while expressing regret for any unintentional error or omission, will be happy to make the necessary correction in future printings. Grateful acknowledgment is made to the following publishers, authors, agents, and estates that have generously granted permission to use quotations from the following copyrighted works.

Abercrombie, Barbara: "What It's Like." Used by permission of the author.

Ackerman, Diane: Excerpt from "Grace" from *Origami Bridges*. Copyright 2002 by Diane Ackerman. Used by permission of HarperCollins Publishers.

Adair, Virginia Hamilton: "The Year After" from *Ants on the Melon: A Collection of Poems*. Copyright 1996 by Virginia Hamilton Adair. Used by permission of Random House, an imprint and division of Penguin Random House LLC. All rights reserved.

Addonizio, Kim: Excerpt from "Death Poem" from *What Is This Thing Called Love: Poems* by Kim Addonizio. Copyright 2004 by Kim Addonizio. Used by permission of W. W. Norton & Company, Inc.

Gallagher, Tess: "Yes" and excerpt from "Sixteenth Anniversary" from *Midnight Lantern: New and Selected Poems*. Copyright 2006 by Tess Gallagher. Reprinted with the permission of The Permissions Company, LLC, on behalf of Graywolf Press, Minneapolis, Minnesota, graywolfpress.org.

Gallmann, Kuki: Excerpts and "*I tuoi occhi eran colore d'acqua* (Your eyes were the colour of water)" from *I Dreamed of Africa*. Copyright 1991 by Kuki Gallmann. Used by permission of Viking Books, an imprint of Penguin Publishing Group, a division of Penguin Random House LLC. All rights reserved.

Gilbert, Elizabeth: Quote from Instagram. Copyright 2018 by Elizabeth Gilbert. Used by permission of The Wylie Agency LLC.

Gilbert, Jack: "Michiko Dead" and "Alone" from *The Great Fires: Poems, 1982–1992*. Copyright 1994 by Jack Gilbert. Used by permission of Alfred A. Knopf, an imprint of the Knopf Doubleday Publishing Group, a division of Penguin Random House LLC. All rights reserved.

Hafiz: "Absolutely Clear" from the Penguin Compass publication *The Subject Tonight Is Love: 60 Wild and Sweet Poems of Hafiz* by Daniel Ladinsky. Copyright 1996, 2003 by Daniel Ladinsky. Used by permission.

Hafner, Katie: Excerpt from *Mother Daughter Me*. Copyright 2013 by Katie Hafner. Used by permission of Random House, an imprint and division of Penguin Random House LLC. All rights reserved.

Haines, John: Excerpt from "For Daphne at Lone Lake" from *Cicada*. Copyright 1977 by John Haines. Used by permission of Wesleyan University Press.

Hall, Donald: Excerpt from *The Best Day the Worst Day*.

Levin, Phillis: "Vigil" from *The Afterimage*, Copper Beech Press. Copyright 1995 by Phillis Levin. Used by permission of the author.

Lewis, C. S.: Excerpts from *A Grief Observed*. Copyright 1961 by C. S. Lewis Pte. Ltd. Used by permission of C. S. Lewis Pte. Ltd.

Lynch, Thomas: "In the Garden" from *Still Life in Milford*. Copyright 1998 by Thomas Lynch. Used by permission of W. W. Norton & Company, Inc.

Maddox, Marjorie: "Elegy for a Man and a House." Copyright 1995 by Marjorie Maddox. Previously published in *Perpendicular As I* and *Beloved on the Earth*, edited by Jim Perlman, Deborah Cooper, Mara Hart, and Pamela Mittlefehldt, Holy Cow! Press. Used by permission of the author.

Malden, Carla: Excerpt from *AfterImage*. Copyright 2011 by Carla Malden. Used by permission of Rowman & Littlefield Publishing Group.

Maynard, Joyce: Excerpt from *The Best of Us*, published by Bloomsbury. Copyright 2018 by Joyce Maynard. Used by permission of the author.

McCarthy, Mary C.: "Husband," originally published in *Beloved on the Earth*, edited by Jim Perlman, Deborah Cooper, Mara Hart, and Pamela Mittlefehldt, Holy Cow! Press. Used by permission of the author.

McDougall, Jo: "Companion," originally published in *The Undiscovered Room*, 2016. Used with permission of Tavern Books.

McKeithen, Madge: Excerpt from "Grief Work" from *Blue Peninsula: Essential Words for a Life of Loss and Change*. Copyright 2006 by Madge McKeithen. Used by permission of Farrar, Straus & Giroux.

Mellon, Emma: "Waking Instructions," originally in *What Have*

Endnotes

p. xviii *"not release from grief"*: Donald Hall, *The Best Day the Worst Day* (New York: Houghton Mifflin, 2005), 118.

p. xviii *"Only grieving heals grief"*: Anne Lamott, personal correspondence with author, May 2020.

p. xviii *"Give sorrow words"*: William Shakespeare, *Macbeth*, act 4, sc. 3.

p. xviii *"We are not good about admitting grief"*: Madeleine L'Engle, *Two-Part Invention* (1998; repr., New York: HarperCollins, 1989), 229.

p. xix *"in allowing ourselves to give exquisite attention"*: Jan Richardson, *The Cure for Sorrow* (Orlando, FL: Wanton Gospeller Press, 2016), 181.

p. xix *"the old words. . . death, grief"*: Julian Barnes, "The Loss of Depth," *Levels of Life* (2013; repr., New York: Vintage, 2014), 77.

p. xix *"the black clay of stubbornness going on after"*: Jane Hirshfield, "Rebus," *Given Sugar, Given Salt* (2001; repr., New York: Harper Perennial, 2002), 12.

p. xix *"slowly the leaves of my life turned"*: Patti Smith, *M Train* (2015; repr., New York: Vintage, 2016), 236.

Index of Authors
and Titles of Works

About the Editor

Barbara Abercrombie has published novels, poetry, children's picture books, including the award-winning *Charlie Anderson*, and books of nonfiction. Two of her books on creative writing are featured on the Best Books for Writers list in *Poets & Writers* magazine. Her personal essays have appeared in national publications as well as in many anthologies. She has received the Outstanding Instructor Award and the Distinguished Instructor Award at UCLA Extension, where she teaches creative writing in the Writers' Program. She lives in Los Angeles and Lake Arrowhead, California.

www.barbaraabercrombie.com